Tottenham & Wood Green

Past & Present

Chris Protz &
Deborah Hedgecock

SUTTON PUBLISHING

Sutton Publishing Limited
Phoenix Mill · Thrupp · Stroud
Gloucestershire · GL5 2BU

First published 2003

Title page: Old Horse Pond at Rectory Farm, White Hart Lane, *c.* 1890. According to Fisk, in hot weather carts passed through the pond to water the horse and dampen the cartwheels to make the spokes swell and prevent them falling out.

British Library Cataloguing in Publication Data
A catalogue record for this book is available from the British Library.

ISBN 0-7509-2986-3

Typeset in 10.5/13.5 Photina.
Typesetting and origination by
Sutton Publishing Limited.
Printed and bound in England by
J.H. Haynes & Co. Ltd, Sparkford.

Mrs Clarke and her daughter-in-law at the stile in White Hart Lane, *c.* 1870. The stile led to Devonshire Hill and Turner's Field, once favoured by courting couples. Mrs Clarke's sons took this photograph, along with many others of the locality. Employed by Saville's, the musical firm near Bruce Grove, they supplemented their income with plate camera photography.

CONTENTS

HAIR CUTTING
SHAVING
SALOONS
CLOTHING DEPARTMENT

L.E. Ward & Co., clothiers, tailors and hosiers, 11 West Green Road, Tottenham, *c.* 1902. The occasion for this highly adorned shop front was possibly to celebrate a victorious end to the Boer War. This establishment belonged to the Ward family. It eventually moved to Seven Sisters Corner to join the other family businesses, becoming Ward's Department Stores.

ACKNOWLEDGEMENTS

The authors would especially like to thank the following for their generosity, help and hard work in completing this book: Lee Arnot, Val Crosby, Jeff Gerhardt, Janet Harris, Henry Jacobs, Rita Read, Jacky Rodger, Bill Rust and Robert Waite.

We have welcomed the encouragement and support from all members of staff and volunteers at Bruce Castle Museum, both past and present, as well as the many respected local historians of the Tottenham and Wood Green area: Albert Pinching, Cate Ablett, Alan Barker, Ken Barker, Maria Basharan, Dorothy Bryan, Rhiannon Cackett, Sylvia Collicott, the late Peter Curtis, the late Frederic Fisk, Ken Gay, Siân Harrington, George Ioannou, Oona Kelly, Derek and Corinne Lewis, Jim Lewis, Lauren Peril (of Lancasterian School), Alan Read, Graham Russell and Hazel Whitehouse.

All modern views were taken by Henry Jacobs, with the exception of those on pages 67 and 73. We are grateful to Tony Gay for permitting us to use his modern-day picture of Tottenham Carnival Parade on page 109. The older pictures, from the end of the nineteenth century, are from a collection of local photographs held in Bruce Castle Museum, Tottenham. They were taken by a number of local photographers, including Frederic Fisk, A. Little and the Hunnings brothers. Copies and originals of Fisk's work were bequeathed to Bruce Castle Museum.

If readers would like to donate original photographs to be added to the Borough's historical collections or lend original photographs for copying, please contact the Curator at Bruce Castle Museum on 020 8808 8772.

INTRODUCTION

Today we are accustomed to streets and houses crowding our landscape, broken by the occasional greenery of parks and open spaces. These green spaces are all that is left of the rural landscape that characterised Tottenham and Wood Green until the nineteenth century. Since then there has been relentless building of streets and houses, shops and offices, factories and workshops, many of which have changed again and again over the past century. The photographs in this book trace some of those changes, contrasting the places we see today with those from the nineteenth and eighteenth centuries.

Tottenham was a very early settlement among the forests on the western bank of the River Lea. By the eighteenth century it was a well-established village, straggling mainly along the old Roman Road out of London to Hertfordshire and East Anglia. To the east of the High Road were the marshy fields and boundary of the River Lea. To the west was the forest from which the settlement had once been carved, and now cleared as far as the remnant of Tottenham Wood. Even this had gone by 1800, to make way for farms around the hamlet of Wood Green. The river, made navigable by the cutting of the River Lea Navigation, together with the road, provided transport links to London, giving rise to a thriving agricultural community, helping to feed the people of London.

Tottenham retained its rural nature, with its farms and nurseries, large houses and coaching inns, until the crowded, narrow streets of London could no longer contain its expanding population and industries. Tottenham's farms and big estates were gradually sold off to speculative builders. The growth of this London suburb was aided by the opening of the Liverpool Street to Enfield railway line in 1872, giving work and market opportunities for the newcomers. Tottenham's population grew by some 60,000 in the second half of the nineteenth century, and a massive 100,000 more in the first three decades of the twentieth century.

Until the end of the nineteenth century Wood Green remained a small hamlet of farms on the rising ground to the west of Tottenham and clustered around the junction between Green Lanes and Lordship Lane. By 1844 its population had grown sufficiently to lead to the building of St Michael's Chapel of Ease along Jolly Butcher's Hill, saving the residents the long walk to the parish church of All Hallows near Bruce Castle. In 1866 it became a parish with the establishment of St Michael's Church, and in 1894 Wood Green gained its independence from Tottenham with the creation of the Urban District Council. The two boroughs then went their separate ways until 1965, when they were rejoined, together with Hornsey, in the London Borough of Haringey.

The two main roads passing through Tottenham and Wood Green have helped define the nature of these emerging communities. The older road, Ermine Street, later Tottenham High Road, established links between Tottenham, the East End and the City of London, with the emphasis on industry and commerce. City merchants made their homes there in the eighteenth century, living in the country and working in the city. A century later, there is a more substantial working- and middle-class population, incomers from London and the countryside. The coming of the railways and the growing population stimulated the establishment of local businesses, such as Harris Lebus and Gestetners in Tottenham Hale and J.A. Prestwich in Northumberland Park.

Green Lanes, passing through Wood Green from Shoreditch to Enfield, was originally part of a series of trackways, used mainly by drovers, until its gradual development as a major highway from the eighteenth century. The establishment of a substantial network of tram services from the end of the nineteenth century, following the opening of the Great Northern Railway King's Cross line in 1850, stimulated links with London and its growth as a commuter suburb. The extension of the Piccadilly Line between the wars, with Turnpike Lane and Wood Green stations, further increased commuter accessibility to London and the West End.

The stories in these photographs take us through the two main thoroughfares that opened up movement into and out of the area, and on to the unfolding of an urban community.

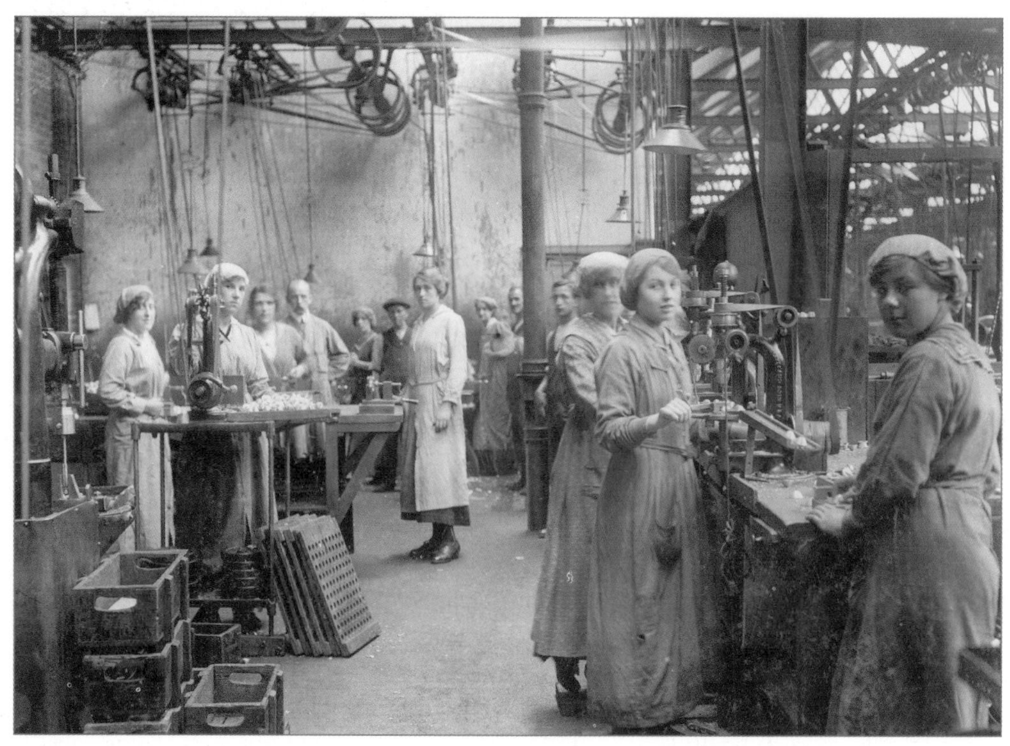

JAP factory munitions workers, Northumberland Park, Tottenham 1914–18. With the onset of the First World War the engineering firm of John A. Prestwich turned to manufacturing munitions as well as aircraft parts and motorcycle engines. With its skilled workforce going off to war, the factory employed women for the first time to work on its production line.

1

Tottenham High Road

Tommy Berry, an itinerant shoe-black, hawking his trade in Tottenham, *c.* 1890. This photograph was part of a series produced by Fred Fisk, whose bookshop and publishing premises were in Tottenham High Road. Tommy would have seen many people passing through Tottenham, as the High Road was a main thoroughfare from the City to Hertfordshire and East Anglia. Long-established coaching inns are placed at strategic points along its length from Stamford Hill to Edmonton, and some of the fine Georgian houses of the eighteenth-century settlement of wealthy City merchants still remain. The High Road also developed extensive shopping parades to meet the needs of people who moved here from London and the country as a whole, as the farms and fields around Tottenham Village passed over to streets and houses during the course of the nineteenth century.

Waggon & Horses public house, 892 Tottenham High Road, *c*. 1905. The Edmonton to Stamford Hill tram stands outside with passengers ready to leave. By 1875 the North Metropolitan Tramways Company had horse tram services running from the City. By the 1880s this had been extended right through Tottenham to Ponders End. After 1904 the entire tramway system in the district was electrified and operated alongside the new motor omnibuses.

Coach & Horses public house, 862 Tottenham High Road, 2002. Although the Waggon & Horses pub no longer exists, early records show both pubs as near neighbours from 1723 onwards. As essential stopping points along the High Road, travellers could tend and water their animals and of course themselves. Well into the nineteenth century the High Road was notoriously ill maintained. The road was made of gravel and after bad weather coaches and carts were known to sink and stick fast in the mud.

Nos 830–8 Tottenham High Road, *c.* 1897. Like many pubs along the High Road, the Roebuck (no. 838) was a former coaching inn. A surviving plan shows a gateway leading off the main road into the Roebuck Yard behind with its stables, coach house, skittle yard and clubroom. Other shops in this parade include Charles Newman's dairy (no. 836), the hairdresser Mrs Ann Jones (no. 834), the boot and shoemaker Samuel Nicholls (no. 832) and Mudie & Kerridge, the children's outfitters (no. 830).

The Roebuck Inn is no longer here but its former existence is now marked by Roebuck Lane. The newer shops that had replaced the old weatherboarded and bow-fronted buildings have in turn been rebuilt, to include today the premises of Keedale Insurance Brokers.

Crowds at Tottenham Hotspur Football Club's stadium, 748 High Road, 1950. With the famous maxim of their manager Arthur Rowe, 'Make it simple, make it quick', Spurs went from strength to strength after the Second World War. The fans hold high their cockerel mascot at Spurs' promotion in 1950. The following year the club won the championship for the first time.

Since the 1950s the stadium has undergone redevelopments to accommodate its increasing number of supporters. The Paxton Road Members' Stand was completed in the 1997/8 season, increasing the ground's capacity to about 36,000. Here, young Spurs fans gather outside in 2002 sporting their team's latest strip.

Dial House, 790 Tottenham High Road, photographed by A. Little in 1892. This building took its name from the sundial placed high on the chimney. Built in 1691 for Moses Trulock, a City soap manufacturer, the house continued to belong to the family until the 1830s.

Although much modernised, Dial House is one of several surviving houses from the Georgian period in the High Road and is Grade II listed.

Glickman's ironmongery, 702–4 Tottenham High Road, *c.* 1933–4. Ironmonger Mr H.A. Dale once owned this shop and installed his blacksmith's forge and workshop to manufacture ironwork. In 1932 the business was sold to Hyman and Annie Glickman and their son Gerald, a Jewish family who owned other shops in the East End. They provided a traditional service, supplying customers with all types of goods for most trades. The motor showrooms next door belong to King's, a long-standing family business of carriage-makers in Tottenham.

Derek Lewis, the current owner, with customers. Derek started work here as a fourteen-year-old and together with wife Corinne has worked at Glickman's ever since. Original fittings of numerous small drawers and pigeon-holes set in a mahogany surround can still be found in the shop. The year 2002 saw Glickman's 75th year of trading – one of the longest-serving businesses on the High Road.

The ornate premises of H. Henderson and Sons, nurserymen, seedsmen and florists, who also owned the Elmhurst Nursery in Cheshunt, 692–4 Tottenham High Road, *c.* 1909. This 'old established seed warehouse' represented the successful market gardening industry of the Tottenham and Lea Valley area.

Local nurseries began to close down as the land was developed for housing. One hundred years later a Turkish restaurant and an Afro-Caribbean food and cosmetic store trade from the same buildings.

Deane's Corner, 665 Tottenham High Road, early 1990s. A Tottenham landmark, Deane's butcher's shop had been run by the same family since 1884. Well into the twentieth century local farms still supplied the shop with meat; livestock were led into the shop and slaughtered at the rear of the premises. The last butcher, Tom Deane, is seen here with one of his oldest customers. The shop closed in 2000 when Tom retired.

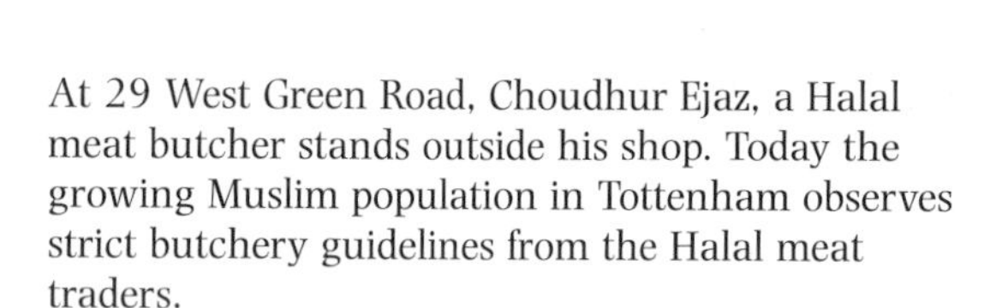

At 29 West Green Road, Choudhur Ejaz, a Halal meat butcher stands outside his shop. Today the growing Muslim population in Tottenham observes strict butchery guidelines from the Halal meat traders.

A roof-top view of the Bell Brewery, Tottenham High Road, showing the old malt loft prior to its demolition in 1926. This view is taken west with a glimpse of the High Road beyond. From 1862 Gripper Brothers owned the Bell Brewery. According to Fisk's *History of Tottenham* (1913), after the terrible thunderstorm and severe flooding of 1878 'one of Mr Gripper's sons amused himself by rowing up and down the High Road in a boat, taking passengers at *6d* each and giving the money to the Tottenham Hospital'.

In 1896 Whitbread & Company transformed the premises into a large bottling depot. In operation until the 1970s, today the old clockface of the Whitbread Brewery is all that remains. This Victorian industrial façade is protected under its Grade II listing. The land currently houses the offices of local charities.

Frederic Fisk, printer and antiquarian bookseller, 605 Tottenham High Road, *c.* 1900. Fisk's own book, *History of Tottenham*, published in 1913, was displayed open in his window, alongside postcards of the district. There was restricted access to the back of Fisk's shop, where he kept rare books and antique prints. Herbert Hawkes recalls the shop as 'dark and musty', and Fisk himself as 'a man in his 60s, grizzled and grey, with steel-rimmed spectacles and wearing a velvet grey smoking hat'. As well as his excellent and well-researched history book, Fisk produced his own local postcards. These were part of a series of *Views of Old Tottenham*, which he later expanded to include Edmonton, Enfield, Waltham Cross and Waltham Abbey: Frederic Fisk left a pictorial record of Tottenham between 1880 and 1910 that can only be envied by other publishers.

Establishing his shop in 1886, Fisk continued trading until 1924 when, following the death of his wife, he closed for business. The shop remained his home until he died in 1935. Fisk's obituary read: 'This neighbourhood has lost one of its "ancient landmarks".' The former parade of shops on the High Road has been completely rebuilt, to be succeeded by Millicent Fawcett Court, a block of council flats.

W.N. Luxford's bakery, 624 Tottenham High Road by Scotland Green, 1905. One local resident recalls her mother trying to make ends meet in the 1920s: 'Us eldest children usually had to go out every morning before school to the baker's in the High Road called Luxford's. And we used to buy a few coppers-worth of stale bread – the previous day's bread – which saw us through that day.'

Luxford's continued baking on the High Road at this shop, as well as at no. 611, for over thirty years. At that same corner today is the local job centre, with the flats of Rheola Court beyond: the name is all that is left of the former Georgian villa, Rheola House, which stood at 630 High Road.

Burgess's Department Store, 578–92 Tottenham High Road, *c.* 1931. Originally trading at 278–92 High Road, this business was acquired (and expanded) by John Petch from Adam Burgess in 1912. Opening in 1924, Burgess's was one of the finest drapery emporiums in North London. Admired for its modern and spacious store layout, arcades, island windows and lighting, it carried the name Sanchez House. This recalled the sixteenth-century Spanish benefactor Balthazar Sanchez, who had built almshouses on this site. Over 300 years old, these dwellings had been declared unfit for habitation in 1905 and were demolished in 1923.

Burgess's Department Store operated for the next sixty years before being replaced by the Co-op (which moved there from its Lansdowne Road premises). Today Sanchez House has been demolished and the supermarket Aldi, its car park and a busy small shopping parade occupy the site.

Offices and showrooms of G.L. Wilson & Co. Ltd, builders' merchants, 522 Tottenham High Road, *c.* 1885. From 1877 this family firm supplied materials to property speculators developing land along the Lea Valley to Hertfordshire. The company had warehouses and depots at all the local stations as well as at Waltham Cross, Enfield, Edmonton and High Barnet.

By about 1905 G.L Wilson had upgraded their showrooms to incorporate new steel-framed windows. A long-standing Tottenham company, Wilson's was still in operation until the 1970s. Today the Iceland store marks the spot. The upper storey retains the original façade of these former offices.

Hay carts drawing into Tottenham High Road, *c.* 1900. Photographed at a time when Tottenham was still rural in parts, the drovers have just steered their loads on to the main road from Reform Row. This was the route from the hay fields by Tottenham Marshes. Carts and other horse-drawn traffic formed ruts in the mud on this busy highway into London.

The junction of Reform Row today divides the hustle and bustle of the High Road from the residential roads of old artisan houses in Tottenham. Some of the residents are related to the families who moved into these houses at the turn of the nineteenth century.

Crowds gather at the decorated railway bridge outside Bruce Grove station by Tottenham High Road to celebrate the opening of the first electric tramline from Wood Green to Tottenham in 1904. Operated by the Metropolitan Electric Tramways (MET), the trams carried passengers from Jolly Butchers Hill in Wood Green via Lordship Lane, down to Bruce Grove.

The station at the corner of Bruce Grove has been here since 1872 following the arrival of the Great Eastern Railway. It was built where the elegant Bruce House once stood on the High Road. Today it is a bustling junction where traffic from the A10 meets the High Road and where commuters pick up the train into Liverpool Street.

Nos 502–8 Tottenham High Road, *c.* 1910. This view of the shops was taken from the railway bridge at Bruce Grove station. Old weatherboarded shops and roadside stalls were replaced by these new buildings in 1907–8. The milliners and children's outfitters Mudie and Kerridge moved here from 830 High Road.

From the same point on the High Road in 2002 can be seen a Turkish jewellers, an electricity showroom, McDonald's restaurant, a telephone shop, the Angelic Hair Salon (that doubles as an evangelistic prayer room) and Percy Ingles the bakers.

Regulars congregate outside the Plough public house, 474 Tottenham High Road, in 1890. Set back off the High Road, this ancient inn was originally built in 1537. Until 1860 the Court Leet for Tottenham held annual meetings here. Prior to 1840 the inn's garden at the rear had a fountain. As local factories demanded ever more water, the fountain soon dried up.

By 1891 the Plough and its neighbouring row of cottages were pulled down, and another building was erected in 1892. Above the bar was a large room called Holcombe Hall, available for dinners, balls and receptions. In March 1962 the pub and shops were demolished, only to be rebuilt in 1963.

Lawson's, saddler's and harness-maker's shop, 450 Tottenham High Road, *c.* 1870. Proprietor Isaac John Lawson (wearing a hat) stands in the road. On the right is his son Isaac, aged seventeen years, with their shop assistant in front of Noble's Clock House. Isaac Senior's sisters look out of the bay window above.

The building at 450 High Road is now Billo Shoes, selling fashionable Italian footwear.

Sergeant Hale of Tottenham police station, High Road, 1909. He wears medals awarded that year for his heroism in the 'Tottenham Outrage', the notorious crime that shocked Edwardian Britain. With other officers and locals Hale chased two armed robbers, narrowly escaping gunshots.

Two of today's police officers walk along the High Road with the Tottenham police station in the background. The current building was constructed in 1914.

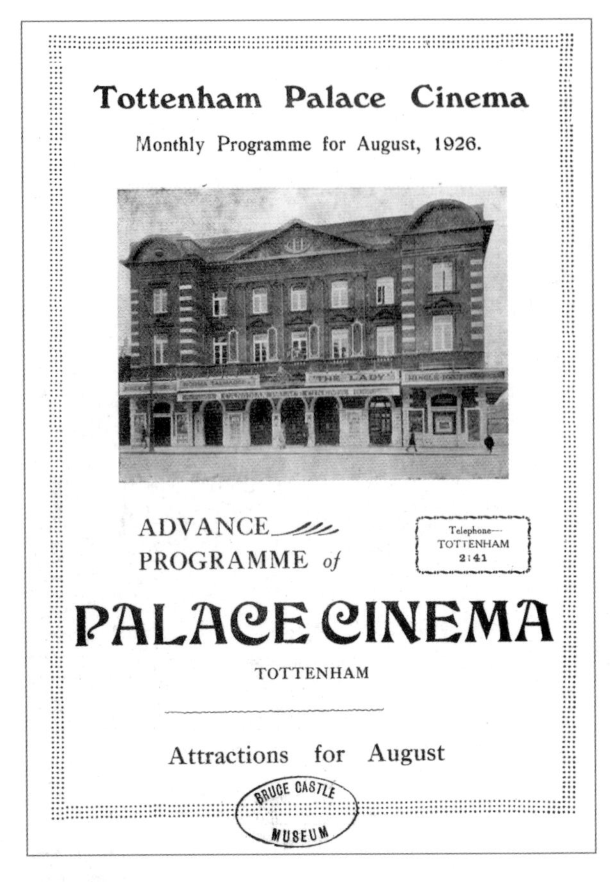

Tottenham Palace Cinema

Monthly Programme for August, 1926.

ADVANCE
PROGRAMME *of*

Telephone—
TOTTENHAM
2141

PALACE CINEMA

TOTTENHAM

Attractions for August

Cinema programme from Tottenham Palace, which was on the west side of Tottenham High Road, 1926. Designed by Eylson and Long, the Palace was built as a variety theatre in 1908 but became a picture house because of the increasing popularity of films. One local recalls the 1920s before the arrival of 'talkies': 'We used to go up to what they called "the gods" in the Palace. We used to go see Charlie Chaplin for 6*d*. All the old films, silent films. All of a sudden the platform would open and the organ would come up from underneath the floor.'

The Palace became a bingo hall in about 1970 and now hosts a charismatic church. With listed-building status, this former theatre remains a treasured landmark for the borough of Haringey.

Tottenham Public Library, High Road, 1905. Built in 1895, this was the main library in Tottenham. Notice Fred Fisk's small shop front to the left of the picture, where he sold his local books and postcards (see also p. 18).

The original building was converted into flats called Library Court in 1994. A new library opened in 1990 at Tottenham Green, named in tribute to the inspirational Black leader Marcus Garvey.

Turner's House, High Cross, Tottenham, before 1881. This remarkable view shows a horse's skeleton over the stables. One of Turner's sons was a vet who saved the displayed horse from a badly broken leg, and for his services he was allowed to keep the horse. When it eventually died he preserved its skeleton as a sign for his veterinary business.

Turner's House was demolished in 1881 and replaced by the unusual houses of Rawlinson's Terrace. The skeleton of the horse was transferred to the opposite side of Tottenham High Road and for many years stood on the hoardings of Colman's premises.

High Cross monument, Tottenham High Road, 1920s. Once believed to be a cross marking the passage of the funeral cortège of Eleanor of Castile in 1290, the origins of the High Cross remain obscure. A wayside marker has been recorded as being on this spot for at least 600 years. Once a wooden monument, the stone cross we recognise today was modified in 1809.

By the twentieth century the High Cross was beginning to lean. Attempts to rectify the tilt were only achieved to any satisfaction in August 1952. With the building of Monument Way, the last twenty-five years has seen this ancient monument positioned on a traffic island.

The Swan public house in 1890. Situated on the corner of Tottenham High Road and Philip Lane, the Swan has served passers-by since about 1455 and is probably the oldest tavern in the district. Notable drinkers include Izaak Walton, the seventeenth-century fisherman of the River Lea, who delightfully records his visit in *The Compleat Angler*. The Swan is described elsewhere as having 'an arbour in front, of such exceeding rural beauty, that it contributed to cheer the senses of travellers, as they sat and invigorated their bodies'.

The Swan of today is scarcely recognisable as the once idyllic tavern of 1890. Its position by the High Cross makes it still a prominent landmark on the High Road as well as the terminus destination of the no. 73 bus route.

Tottenham Bus Garage, Philip Lane, *c.* 1913. In 1910 the first reliable and efficient motorised buses went into service. Within a year the familiar horse buses had disappeared. By 1913 the MET, fearing competition elsewhere, formed their own motor bus company – the Tramways (MET) Omnibus Company. Their new garage at Tottenham is shown here.

The MET was soon taken over by the London General Omnibus Company (which had previously operated the horse buses). The bus garage has stood on this same site next door to the Swan pub for almost 100 years. It is now run by the Arriva Bus Company.

The Prince of Wales Hospital, Tottenham Green, 1947. Dr Laseron established the Tottenham Deaconess Institute here in 1869. With their distinctive black uniforms, the Deaconesses trained nurses and cared for the sick. Following Dr Laseron's death in 1894, the Institute became a general hospital and was opened by the Prince and Princess of Wales in 1907. Over the years the hospital expanded, buying up land and converting adjoining properties to become a valuable local resource.

Despite widespread campaigning to save it, the hospital was forced to close in 1985. The attractive frontage, with its ornate adornment of the carved plumes of the Prince of Wales, has been preserved following the building's conversion into flats in 1993. Known as Deaconess Court, it recalls the name of the first nurses who provided training here.

Fred Fisk's photograph of a road worker and steamroller, Tottenham Green, in 1886.

In 2002 the same stretch of road, from the Seven Sisters tube station through Tottenham Green to the High Cross, underwent major resurfacing of the bus lane.

FURNISHING
239
241 CABINET
SHOW ROOMS
WARD'S
BROADWAY
FURNISHING
STORES
WARD'S
BROADWAY
FURNISHING
STORES
WARD'S
BROADWAY
STORES
SUITE 8

Ward's Stores Ltd, Seven Sisters Corner, Tottenham High Road, *c.* 1905. This store began when the family-owned business acquired a house in 1901 and gradually took over the entire parade. A department store, it sold furniture, furnishings and jewellery. Shoppers paid for their goods via a central payment control system. The corner building still retains its original steel-framed windows, possibly the first of their type in Tottenham. To this day the area is often referred to as 'Ward's Corner'.

Ward's Stores closed its doors in June 1972. Now Seven Sisters Market, an array of businesses from Colombian coffee shops, Caribbean food stalls and luggage shops serve the local community and passing trade to and from the nearby tube station.

A no. 643 trolleybus at the junction of Broad Lane and Tottenham High Road, 1961. These vehicles adapted the existing tramway facilities, but were considered to have the same disadvantages as the trams before them. Trolleybuses were discontinued in July 1961, to be replaced by the familiar Routemaster buses.

In 2002 a great number of buses still followed the red bus lane outside the former Barclays Bank (now a listed building) and Tesco in the High Road.

2

Wood Green High Road

Two soldiers, part of a colonial regiment from West Africa, passing through Wood Green in 1902. They had been billeted at Alexandra Palace for a month, together with other regiments taking part in the parade and celebrations for Edward VII's coronation. Alexandra Palace, described as the 'Palace for the People', was designed for exhibitions and entertainment on the lines of the Crystal Palace, and opened in 1873 on former farmland of Tottenham Wood Farm. The two men are standing on Wood Green High Road near Noel Park Road, on their way from the Palace to Noel Park station. Noel Park was on a branch line opened in 1878, linking Alexandra Palace (at Palace Gates station) with Liverpool Street via Seven Sisters in Tottenham. The line closed in 1964; together with the Great Northern main line from King's Cross, it was part of the substantial transport network, including trams and buses, opening up Wood Green for workers, shoppers and leisure seekers.

Green Lanes, Harringay, in about 1925, showing a Harrod's van opposite the dining-rooms. Green Lanes was part of a series of trackways running from Shoreditch to Enfield and on to Hertford, developing into a major highway by the eighteenth century. From the end of the nineteenth century the growing community of Harringay gave rise to parades of shops along this stretch known as Grand Parade.

The emptiness of the pre-war scene above, with its delivery van and tram, contrasts with the 2002 scene of a traffic-congested main road. However, Green Lanes continues to be a vibrant shopping area of local, small shops, reflecting the Greek and Turkish contribution to the district. In particular, the food shops, including specialist grocery stores and mouth-watering Eastern Mediterranean patisseries, invite shoppers from far away.

This elegant parade, featuring the Salisbury Hotel seen here in 1912, looks north along Green Lanes to the newly built Coliseum Cinema. This cinema, with its distinctive rounded façade, was a popular venue until after the Second World War, but was converted into a bingo hall in 1961. The Salisbury, which boasted a large ballroom, was opened in 1899.

The shops at ground level have been modernised, but their upper storeys and the Salisbury Hotel on the corner, with its magnificent curved frontage, have retained their original architecture. The old Coliseum has now been demolished following a period of disuse, and this picture shows construction in progress for the new Coliseum Apartments.

A few pedestrians amble across the empty spaces of Turnpike Lane where it meets Green Lanes, helped rather unnecessarily (we might think) by a policeman. Behind them are the houses of Newent and Pleasant Villas. Built in 1850, the buildings shown here were photographed just before demolition in 1931, to make way for the new Turnpike Lane station.

Turnpike Lane station was opened in 1932 as part of the extension to the Piccadilly Line. The station created easier access for work, leisure and shopping for the people of Wood Green and the surrounding area and stimulated the development of more homes. It included a shopping parade and a cinema, but the cinema was demolished in 1999 to make way for a substantial extension to the bus garage.

The Wellington public house, seen here in 1903, dominates the corner where Green Lanes meets Turnpike Lane and was well located for travellers as well as the local community. The houses alongside give the appearance of a suburban road but for the electric tram making its way along Green Lanes. From this point to Palmers Green, Green Lanes becomes Wood Green High Road.

Present-day travellers are now as likely to want a quick meal from a fast food outlet. We can still see the main building of the old Wellington, with the addition of an extension on the left-hand side. Shops replaced the Victorian houses during the 1930s, including the art deco building of Montague Burton with a Temperance billiard hall above and Times Furniture Store. Both have since changed hands.

Marks & Spencer at 44 and 46 Wood Green High Road, shown here in about 1934. M&S originally opened in 1914 as the Penny Bazaar further down the High Road at Cheapside. In 1927 it moved to join the parade of large shops at the beginning of the High Road, with Woolworths at nos 48 and 50 and the large family-owned department store of Barton's at 26–34.

The modern Marks & Spencer is in the same place along the High Road as its 1930s predecessor, although considerably expanded. It lost its neighbouring department store, Barton's, when it closed down after a serious fire in the 1960s, and Woolworths has also moved out and is now located in the Shopping City. However, other chain stores, including British Home Stores and Mothercare, have taken their place.

The Wine Merchants, sometimes known as the 'round house', on the corner of Mayes Road and Wood Green High Road, *c.* 1901. At this point, where Mayes and Alexandra Roads met the High Road, there were the open-fronted shops and stalls of Market Terrace. Local residents have strong memories of the lively market, with its cheaply priced clothes, books and china stalls, as well as the greengrocers and fishmongers displaying their produce on the stalls outside.

Throughout the twentieth century Wood Green developed into a main shopping centre for many nearby districts, and an additional boost was given with the building of the Wood Green Shopping City in 1981. The 'City' replaced the shops in the picture above, and was further extended by using the railway land on both sides of the High Road vacated by the closure of the Palace Gates branch line.

Lipton's provision stores, with the manager, William Cuthill and his staff, *c.* 1909. In the 1890s William Cuthill and five other men came down from Glasgow, where Thomas Lipton had his first stores, to open shops in London. William Cuthill, wearing dark trousers, is seen standing next to the cashier, Nancy Jacobs, whom he later married. The huge gaslamps of the shop, alongside the hanging rolls and sides of bacon, would have lit up the front on the late evenings of Saturdays and Christmas Eve, when the shop stayed open until everything was sold. Some of the goods, such as the bacon and eggs, were sold directly from the front.

Alexandra Park Tavern, seen here in about 1900, opposite Mayes Road, was established in the 1860s. Originally there were extensive tea gardens alongside, but by the turn of the twentieth century these were lost to the development of Lipton's, Edmond's the large drapery store and Boots the Chemist. The single-storey extension on the front was added at the time.

Alexandra Tavern survived until the development of the Shopping City in the 1970s, when shops such as Boots and the Co-operative Society, as well as many smaller traders, were demolished to make way for this modern parade on the east side of the High Road. This parade is linked with the development on the other side of the road by a covered arcade to make Wood Green Shopping City.

Dovecot Villas on the east side of the High Road shown prior to demolition in 1910. The houses were part of a row of twelve pairs of Victorian villas built in 1862. Their large gardens fronted the High Road and behind were the fields of Duckett's Farm. Then, from 1881, the substantial Noel Park Estate, offering low-cost housing, was developed on the farmland. By 1910 the house on the left had become the rent and repairs office for the estate, and the one of the right was the Will-Pleeze Laundry.

The shops of Cheapside, showing the Halifax Building Society. Cheapside was the name given to the parade of shops developed by Noel Park Estate and since further modernised.

The entrance to Wood Green Empire in Lymington Avenue, *c.* 1925, part of the Cheapside development. The Empire was a highly successful music hall and variety venue, with a London-wide reputation. It resisted commercial pressure to become a cinema, and staged live shows until the 1950s, with its last performance in January 1955. By this time the building had become very neglected.

For a period during the 1950s and 1960s Wood Green Empire was used as a studio by Associated Television for programmes such as *Emergency Ward 10*. However, substantial redevelopment and improvements of Cheapside and the theatre have since taken place. The Halifax building incorporates the lofty frontage of the Empire building, while round the corner in Lymington Avenue a modern Sainsbury's replaced the main theatre and side entrance.

Spouters Corner on the left of the picture, where Lordship Lane meets Wood Green High Road, was an area of common land popular with political groups and orators who spouted their ideas; now they are usually to be found on the forecourt outside the Central Library. This 1906 picture shows one of the earliest electric trams and on the right the Nag's Head public house. The trees on the right front the gardens of The Elms, a large detached house built in the nineteenth century.

The Nags Head public house on the right is the same building, now smartened and modernised but with a change of name to the Goose in late twentieth-century style. A Safeways store has replaced the shops to the left of Nags Head, and in 1934 the Elms made way for more shops and the Gaumont Palace Theatre. The Gaumont is an impressive art deco building that seats over 2,500, and is currently Grade II listed. It was converted to a bingo hall in 1984, but is now disused.

In 1907 Wood Green Public Library on the corner of Station Road was opened from funding through the foundation of Andrew Carnegie, a Scottish-born philanthropist who supported educational and learning institutions, in this case at a cost of £8,569. With its dark-red brickwork, clock and cupola, it was a notable landmark for residents and passers-by. One local resident has fond memories of Saturday visits in the 1920s and '30s, during his childhood, to choose books, read the *Children's Newspaper* and *Boy's Own* paper in the reading room and obtain information for competitions from the reference room upstairs.

Wood Green Library was demolished in 1973 and moved to modern premises next to the Shopping City. The office block replacing it, with its copper-coloured reflective windows, dominates the corner leading up to Jolly Butchers Hill on the right, although the spire of St Michael's parish church in the distance recalls some of the older scene.

The people peering into these shop windows were looking at the sale goods on offer as the stores faced demolition in 1930 for the building of Wood Green underground station. This parade of shops, formerly known as Hardy Terrace, was built in the 1880s, when the first development of the High Road shops started from Truro Road, north of White Hart Lane.

Wood Green station was built in 1932 as part of the extension of the Piccadilly Line from Finsbury Park to Cockfosters. All the stations on the line, Wood Green included, were designed by Charles Holden, and built in the art deco style. Unfortunately the intended impact of the building is partially obscured by the remaining terrace of Victorian shops.

Hardy Terrace was only partly demolished, and re-emerged round the corner in Lordship Lane. The premises at this time (about 1930) included The People's Teeth Association (Dentist), dining-rooms and Barclays Bank. On the right, there are the premises of Burridges the undertakers, with the pointed roof of Wood Green Congregational chapel, opened in 1864, beyond. The skyline is criss-crossed with the power lines for the electric trams.

The side of Wood Green underground station has replaced the shops in the picture above and the bank is in a new building. Even more dramatic, the modern cinema and restaurant complex of Hollywood Green has replaced the undertakers (relocated to Bounds Green Road), but Wood Green chapel can still be seen in the background, although it is currently disused.

The importance of substantial transport links through Wood Green is shown with this 1910 picture of the tram depot along Jolly Butchers Hill. Opened in 1890 by North Metropolitan Tramways for horse-drawn trams, it was converted in 1904 to take electric trams. The routes from this depot included Finsbury Park, Bruce Grove, Bounds Green, New Southgate, Palmers Green and Enfield. Between 1936 and 1939 the trams were replaced with electric trolleybuses.

The old tram depot had many periods of restructuring to accommodate new-style vehicles, and now Wood Green bus garage is a major depot for North London buses. The London Passenger Transport Board took over from the North Metropolitan Tramways in the 1930s, and the depot is currently managed by Arriva. The trolleybuses continued to be part of the fleet until 1961, when they were replaced by diesel buses.

Adorning the side of Watson's Road are the magnificently ornate Edwardian gaslamps of the Three Jolly Butchers Hotel, a coaching inn from the eighteenth century but rebuilt in about 1900. This little road, shown here in 1910, was once a cul-de-sac. It was named after the Watson family who ran the Jolly Butcher for a number of decades in the nineteenth century. They also owned the fields around the inn, and by 1863 had built ten houses in Watson's Road.

The new office block and modernised public house (now Monaghan's Tavern) have replaced the ornate splendour of the Jolly Butchers Hotel. Watson's Road itself has lost its few houses, and is lined by offices, including the offices for Arriva. On the right is the large office block that replaced the old Printers' Almshouses (built on Watson family land) in the 1970s (see p. 60).

The shops along Church Hill present a crowded scene with shoppers and passers-by posing for this photograph, *c.* 1906. The premises of William Nodes the undertakers on the corner can be seen appropriately next to John Coles, tobacconist, and H.L. Starkey, wine, spirit and beer merchant. Church Hill, named after St Michael's Church on the corner of Bounds Green Road, is more often referred to as Jolly Butchers Hill after the local public house.

The buildings are still recognisable today. The shops, and their frontages, have changed, but the upper storeys are much the same. On the far right we can see part of Wood Green underground station that has replaced some of this parade of shops.

Bounds Green Road, leading off Green Lanes towards Southgate, was once dominated at its entrance by this 21ft obelisk, with its drinking fountain and animal water trough. It was erected in 1879 by Thomas Bywaters Smithies to commemorate the life and work of his mother, Catherine Smithies, an ardent campaigner for animal welfare and temperance. Here we see the obelisk being moved in 1904 to make way for electric tramlines along Bounds Green Road.

The obelisk has been moved further along Bounds Green Road to the green in front of the Prince of Wales public house on the corner of Finsbury Road and Trinity Road. The Prince of Wales, built in about 1870, was once at the top of a parade of shops and houses that extended along Finsbury Road to Nightingale Road. The green, part of Trinity Gardens, is the remnant of common land running alongside Bounds Green Road.

During the nineteenth century there were a number of almshouses built in the semi-rural districts of Wood Green and Tottenham by City companies. The Fishmongers' and Poulterers' Almshouses, shown here in about 1905, were built in 1849 along the High Road opposite White Hart Lane. Close by, on the corner of Bounds Green Road, were the Printers' Almshouses, built in 1856 and demolished in 1970.

The 1960s building of Haringey Civic Centre has now replaced the Tudor-style architecture of the Fishmongers' Almshouses. The Civic Centre was built in 1956 as a town hall for Wood Green, and became Haringey Civic Centre with the amalgamation of Tottenham, Wood Green and Hornsey. The main council chamber and the open curved staircase in the entrance hall are two particularly striking features of the Centre.

The development of Wood Green High Road as a shopping area started north of White Hart Lane in the 1880s, when it was referred to as the High Street. This parade of shops between Nightingale and Truro Roads is shown in 1903. The trees on the left front the gardens of the Nightingale Tavern, with its Masonic Hall and Assembly Rooms, established in 1866.

This shopping parade is one of the last survivors of the large community of small shops established north of White Hart Lane at the end of the nineteenth century. We can see evidence of modernisation and redevelopment, but the last block on the right looks substantially the same, as is the building next to it with its set-back upper storeys. The Nightingale Tavern has been drastically changed and reduced to a single-storey building.

Wood Green station in Buckingham Road was opened in 1859 on the GNR line from King's Cross to the north. In this picture of about 1905 we can see the delivery cart belonging to Edmonds' Bros and Denham & Goyder. Edmonds' was to become one of the earliest department stores in Wood Green. Alongside the station are premises for G.L. Wilson, the Tottenham building firm. On the right is the Alexandra Palace Railway Hotel fronting Avenue Gardens.

The modern picture is surprisingly unchanged. The station has been renamed Alexandra Palace station, but it still overlooks a network of lines, both commuter and inter-city. The Alexandra Palace Hotel also had a name change, in 1958, to the Starting Gate, in recognition of the racecourse established in 1868 in Alexandra Park and closed in 1970. Avenue Gardens, although not shown in this picture, remains a pleasant open space to the right.

3

Links Between the Communities

White Hart Lane in 1912 presents a distinctly rural scene. The lane winds its way gently uphill from Tottenham to Wood Green, an early northern link between the village and the hamlet. By 1912 each end of White Hart Lane had a substantial amount of house building where it met the Tottenham and Wood Green High Roads, but the central part remained farmland until the building of the London County Council and local Council estates in the 1930s. White Hart Lane was one of several lanes and roads linking the farms and hamlets of Tottenham and Wood Green from east to west. Lordship Lane, formerly Berry Lane, ran from Bruce Castle, the former manor house, to Wood Green Common, and West Green Road linked the High Cross with Duckett's Common, passing through West Green at its junction with Philip Lane. Further north, Hanger Lane (now St Ann's Road) led from Stamford Hill to Bean's Green. These are old lanes, pre-dating the seventeenth century, and some parts retained their rural aspects into the twentieth century. However, one new thoroughfare was built, Seven Sisters Road in 1833, starting from Broad Lane, Tottenham, and passing at the very southern end of Harringay.

Seven Sisters Road, Tottenham, *c.* 1910. Named after the landmark seven trees at Page Green off Tottenham High Road, Seven Sisters Road was laid out to make better connections with central London. Only when the railway stations appeared from 1872 did substantial building developments follow. The beer retailer, Whitehead's, stood on the corner of Moreton Road. In the far distance (right) is the Woodberry Tavern (dating from 1879), a former gin palace and hotel. The proprietor Mr Wood had built some of the shops here, in about 1880, although at the time it was thought there were far too many for the needs of the residents.

Tower blocks now peer over the rooftops but little has changed in the same view today. Seven Sisters Road remains an important and very busy thoroughfare. The Woodberry can still be recognised by its exuberant façade. Local residents in the surrounding streets and estates are served by the Victoria Line at Seven Sisters tube station to the north. Opening in 1968, this was the first tube route built since 1907.

Night-time view of Seven Sisters Road, Tottenham, *c.* 1950. Tramlines and overhead wires gleam in the lamplight of fifty years ago. In 1952, when trams were all but phased-out, the nation looked to Tottenham, as a newly designed machine – the Juggernaut – was demonstrated to tear up disused tramway tracks. The recovering of this valuable scrap metal was said to be urgent owing to a countrywide need to support the arms and export industries.

Compared to the deserted street of fifty years ago, the same night-time view is more difficult to photograph today, as the road is in constant use by night buses and traffic.

Hanger Farm, St Ann's Road, Tottenham, photographed by A. Little in March 1891. The road is merely a mud track in this rural area. The farm stood on the north side, to the west of Blackboy Lane. Originally St Ann's Road was called Hanger Lane but it became known as Cut-Throat-Lane after a man committed suicide nearby. Residents petitioned successfully to change the name to St Ann's Road in 1870, after the church that had been built for their community in 1860.

Woodlands Park Board School opened in 1900 in St Ann's Road on this former farmland. Separate buildings on the same site still house Woodlands Park Infants and Junior School.

West Green Road, Tottenham, 1908. View looking west from Tottenham High Road towards the bridge carrying the Great Eastern Railway line. A favourite shopping venue for the working classes, these Edwardian shops include Nolan Denney Provisions Merchants with its large gaslamps (no. 27); the butcher's Edward Coates (no. 29); Giosue Olgiati's restaurant (no. 33); and the stationer's George Warbey, under the bookseller sign (no. 40). The shops kept long hours but were open especially late on a Saturday evening when meat was sold off cheaply: few butchers had cold stores to keep meat fresh over the weekend.

West Green Road remains a lively shopping location. This same stretch today includes Celebrations Party Ware (no. 34), the estate agents Cousins (no. 13), 1st Class Estates (no. 26a) and Castle's (no. 44), the Mauri Asia Post (no. 15) and Tottenham Town Bakery (no. 38). The road reputedly boasts the highest density of speciality fish shops in London. In 1965 no. 43 also witnessed the beginnings of the internationally successful Dyke & Dryden Company, which manufactured Black hair care and beauty products.

MAKERS OF THE "GOODW
96
Cycle Manufacturers
MATTHEW
& at 8, Woodford Rd. Fores
OLD MACHINES TAKEN
IN PART PAYMENT
REPAIRS IN A
BRANCH
Humbers
£10.10.0

CYCLES
ACCESS

Matthews Brothers' bicycle and sport accessories shop, 96 West Green Road, Tottenham, *c.* 1906. A local advert runs, 'For ease, comfort, and durability, ride Goodwin's Cycles. Nothing better made. A marvel of cheapness, made only by Matthews Bros., at their steam works.' Manufacturing all the machines on site, the firm also operated in Forest Gate. From 1909 they supplied rollerskates in response to the new 'rinking' or rollerskating craze. The Canadian Rink opened on Tottenham High Road in February 1910. At 6*d* a session, this was beyond the reach of most children, who opted for skating on the streets.

Today Matthews Brothers is a carpet shop.

No. 198 West Green Road, Tottenham, *c.* 1910. This end-of-terrace house formed part of Troon Villas and was the premises of builder and decorator Mr J.E. Green. Alongside was a piece of land where West Green nurseries and an old villa called the Gothic House could be found. Each year Sanger's circus used this open space as their winter quarters before their summer tour.

Green's became an established Tottenham building firm, remaining in West Green until the early 1970s and continuing in Lordship Lane until about 1989. Today the motor engineers HBS occupies nos 196–8. The piece of land has now been built on with the houses of Mansfield Avenue and Bourn Avenue.

Lock-up store and pavement display of second-hand goods, 376 West Green Road, Tottenham, *c.* 1947. Adjoining houses were demolished from 1950 onwards, along with the lock-up, to make way for the building of the new Catholic church of St John Vianney and its parish hall. The temporary church can be seen behind the hedge.

From 1927 parishioners of St John Vianney used their temporary church for worship. While raising funds for a new building, a Nissen hut was added in 1951. The foundation stone for the new church was laid by the Archbishop of Westminster in April 1958. The official opening was celebrated with High Mass by Father Cuming on Sunday 19 April 1959. The church has been the centre of Catholic life in West Green ever since.

Old Pond and the Bricklayers' Arms public house, West Green, Tottenham, *c.* 1875. This idyllic view by Fisk accompanies his recollection of the horse pond with its wooden posts and rails, left open for horses and carts to pass through. It was a scene that was to rapidly change. The Bricklayers' Arms was demolished, making way for West Green station and the railway line from Seven Sisters to Palace Gates (the service began on 1 January 1878). West Green's population rose rapidly as a consequence. In 1840 there were barely 90 inhabitants; by 1884 over 400 were living there.

West Green station has long gone following the closure of the railway line on 5 January 1963. This area, where Philip Lane meets West Green Road, is now a grassy traffic island. To the north of the road lies Downhills Park and the various buildings of Downhills School.

Rectory Farm, White Hart Lane, Tottenham, 2 January 1894. Also known as Thompson's Farm, after the family who resided there for over 150 years, this view looking eastwards was taken by local photographer A. Little. The farmhouse and barns stood on the south side, with the pond opposite stretching halfway across the lane. After heavy rains the pond often reached the house making it difficult for passers-by to negotiate.

In the 1920s Rectory Farm was one of the last working farms in Tottenham. The pond was filled in not long after, although locals still enjoyed walks through fields up to Weir Hall, Edmonton. Council housing of the Weir Hall 'cottage estate', bounded by Weir Hall Road and White Hart Lane, has occupied the site since the 1930s. The extensive Tottenham Cemetery lies to the south.

Grocery store of Joseph Richard Bray, 5 Bruce Castle Parade, Lordship Lane, Tottenham, *c.* 1906. Standing by Lordsmead Road, this corner shop was much in demand in the days before refrigerators, as shopping was a daily or twice-daily event. In one of his books local historian Herbert Hawkes recounts how, as a young schoolboy at nearby Risley School, he used to run to this corner shop in his lunch hour to buy *2d* blocks of Foster Clark's soups.

Nowadays the Golden Gloves Fitness Centre and AKA minicab firm have their premises in this former Edwardian shopping parade. Together with neighbouring shops, they serve the surrounding residential streets and estates.

Lordship Lane in Wood Green in 1913, showing the premises of E. Burridge, the undertakers (established in 1850) with the farrier's H.D. Chesser (founded in 1770) on the right. This later became Willis & Son seed merchants, with its plant stalls on the open space of Spouters Corner (see p. 52). 'It was a breath of the countryside,' one local resident recalls. Further down we can see the Cinematograph Theatre, one of three Wood Green cinemas opened in 1910. It closed in the late 1920s to became a furniture depository, with Harry Boults School of Dancing on the first floor.

The old Cinematograph building, undertakers and market stalls that replaced Willis's, were demolished in 1999 to make way for the cinema and restaurant complex of Hollywood Green. In the distance there is the old Wood Green Congregational chapel on the corner of Redvers Road, opened in 1864, and now empty after a period as Haringey Arts Centre.

All Hallows Church, Tottenham, seen across the fields of Church Farm from Lordship Lane, *c.* 1880. This view would not have changed much from the time of the first parish church of All Saints during the twelfth century. The church was re-dedicated to All Hallows in the fifteenth century, but the tower dates from the fourteenth. The remainder of the building has undergone various alterations including substantial refurbishments by William Butterfield in 1875. The translator of the King James Bible, William Bedwell, was vicar here between 1607 and 1632.

The same view is obscured today by housing developments and light industry on the north side of Lordship Lane. Nearby Tower Gardens Estate was built in 1910 by the London County Council and was Britain's second municipal 'cottage estate'. The Peabody Estate immediately to the east was completed in 1907. All Hallows remains an active parish church, and, despite the modern world, retains a rural charm. A listed building, it is one of only two surviving medieval churches in Haringey.

East wing of Bruce Castle, Lordship Lane, Tottenham, 1892. This former manor house dates from the Tudor period. The east wing was added in the eighteenth century by the then owner James Townsend. By 1892 Bruce Castle had just closed as a respected progressive school for boys. The school had been established in 1827 and was run by the Hill family. Its most famous former headmaster was Sir Rowland Hill, who created the penny post. Here, Mr Hankin (members of whose family had worked at the school) poses on the path with two workmen.

Bruce Castle and its grounds were purchased by the Tottenham Urban District Council and were opened to the public 'forever' on 13 August 1892. The Museum opened in 1906. Today Bruce Castle is recognised as a Grade I listed building and is still home to Haringey's local history museum and archive. The council's gardeners maintain the historic park of 20 acres. Mark Bambridge (behind) and (from left to right) Mike Best, Joseph Ajayi, Keith Dyer and John Austin.

Broadwaters Farm, Lordship Lane, Tottenham, *c.* 1880. For centuries known as Broadwaters, this small agricultural district gets its name from the flood waters of the Moselle brook (see p. 96). The Moselle frequently flooded its banks here, producing good meadowland and crops of hay for dairy farming. The ivy-clad farmhouse stood on this narrow country lane from about 1798, when it was the home of the Phillips family. They extended the house considerably, using the builder Hobson, who built the Martello towers along the southern coast of England.

Broadwaters dairy farm ceased to operate in 1916. By 1932 Tottenham Urban District Council had acquired the land, pulling down the old farmhouse and constructing the open-air Lido. Amounting to almost 100 acres, this farmland became Lordship Recreation Ground and allotments. In 1940 Rowland Hill School was built to the east. The allotments remained until the towers of Broadwater Farm housing estate replaced them in the 1970s. In this 2002 photograph, flats of Moira Close occupy the site of the former lido.

4

Homes

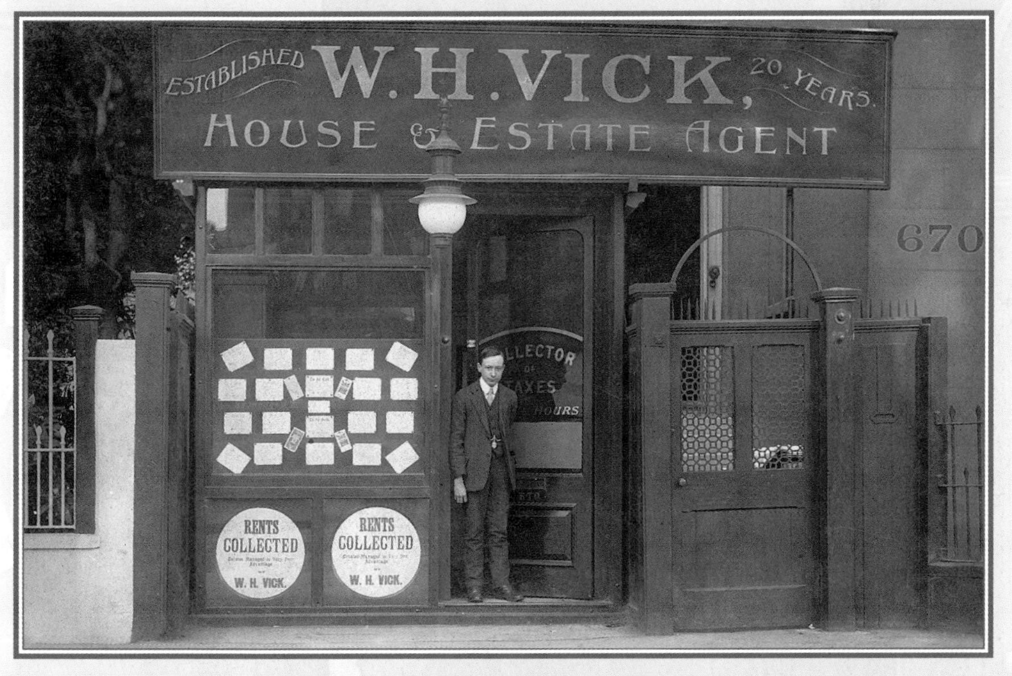

Vick Estate Agents in 1912, showing the 'office boy', Mr Vaughan. Vick's had been established for twenty years by this date, and was one of the many firms of estate agents managing the development of new housing in Tottenham and Wood Green. Most houses were built for let rather than purchase, and in some cases the estate agents managed the collection of rents and repairs of the buildings, although not many houses were kept in a good state of repair. From the second half of the nineteenth century there was a steady erosion of open land, as farms, nurseries and the estates around the larger houses were sold off for development, usually in individual plots or groups of plots to small builders, who built perhaps two or three houses at a time. As a result, many apparently uniform terraced houses in rows of streets actually differ in a variety of ways.

Waggon Lane, Tottenham, *c.* 1932. This narrow road was on the Tottenham/Edmonton border, extending from Tottenham High Road to Willoughby Lane, and was originally known as Waggon Horse Lane. The 1851 census shows a sizeable Irish community living here. The cramped, slum conditions of these homes were a far cry from the genteel opulence of Brook House and its gardens owned by the Klemantaski family, situated (until 1956) only on the other side of the High Road.

Residents of the twenty-seven houses at the High Road end of Waggon Lane were moved into new housing in 1932, following a slum clearance order under the 1930 Housing Act. The area was demolished in 1934. In 2002 Waggon Lane still exists with newer housing, off Brantwood Road.

Cottages off Factory Lane, near Tottenham High Road, 1908. Despite their close proximity to Warne's India Rubber Factory, these long cottage gardens bloomed with flowers and vegetables. Benefitting from the fertile soil of the area, they are a reminder of the large nurseries and farmland that once flourished here.

Today modern flats stand on the former cottage gardens.

Bruce Grove in 1880. This view shows fishmonger Mr Firmer driving his horse and trap with the white-bearded Mr Hinde looking on. The latter was the brother-in-law of the Quaker Dr May. These desirable residences of local Quakers (nos 1–16) were built between 1785 and 1820. With its elm trees and colony of crows, Bruce Grove was a famous North London beauty spot. Following the coming of the railway in 1872, this was all to gradually disappear with the advance of newer housing developments. The billboard points to affordable houses in Moorfield Road.

Beyond the long-established Italian restaurant of San Marco, the Georgian houses still stand and are Tottenham's largest group of listed buildings. In April 2002 a blue plaque was unveiled on 7 Bruce Grove to commemorate the 'Father of Meteorology' Luke Howard (1772–1864) who had lived there. Through his studies of the weather, he created the cloud classification scheme used in forecasting today.

Reynardson's Almshouses, Tottenham High Road, 1937. Built in 1737, this row of eight dwellings and a chapel provided housing for 'four poor men and four poor women' in Tottenham. Two inscriptions over the door record the name of Nicholas Reynardson, the local wealthy merchant, whose bequest of 1685 made this possible.

The sale of the almshouses was authorised in 1938. Still unsold in 1939, the land was requisitioned for Civil Defence during the Second World War. Once the almshouses were demolished the flats of Reynardson Court were erected in 1951, next to the police station. The Reynardson commemorative plaque from the almshouses survives at Bruce Castle Museum.

Albert Place, off Tottenham High Road, 1893. Workmen pose outside the cottages just before repairing the buildings. Past occupants of the cottages were families of workers at the nearby Warne's India Rubber Factory or manual labourers, but also included a butler, a footman, a governess and a minister's wife.

Albert Place today is a small passageway between Peacock's clothes store and the HSBC bank on Tottenham High Road. It leads to the Destiny Centre, one of a number of evangelist churches found in Haringey.

Station Road, leading from Wood Green High Road towards Wood Green station, in 1903, showing the ramshackle weatherboarded shop of a confectioner's with J. Gear, timber merchant behind. The shop was recorded as early as 1837. The tall houses alongside were known as the Jolly Anglers Cottages, with the Jolly Anglers public house, before it was rebuilt in 1905, at the end.

The 1930s Northmet House (belonging to the North Metropolitan Electric Power Supply Co.) and a modern office block have replaced the shops and houses in the above picture, as well as the former Elms Cottages. Northmet House is now Haringey Council offices. The Jolly Anglers maintains its position at the end.

Leading off Station Road are the handsome Dutch gabled houses of Buckingham Road, *c*. 1905. They stand opposite Wood Green station, with the Alexandra Palace Railway Hotel on the corner. The hotel was originally the Palace Café (1875), changed its name in 1958 (see p. 62, bottom). The hansom cabs waiting in the road for passengers coming out of the station are in front of the premises of W. Parker, the job-master at Wood Green station.

The houses remain unchanged, their frontages smartened with fresh paintwork. To the right, replacing W. Parker's premises in the picture above is the Wood Green post office sorting depot, built in 1952.

Bradley Terrace, White Hart Lane, in 1895 was at the edge of Wood Green housing development at this time. Opposite the terrace was White Hart Lane elementary school, opened in 1884, and behind there was the estate of Pellat, Ewart and Williams Groves. On the other side of the terrace, towards Tottenham, White Hart Lane rambled past fields and nurseries, and the two old-established pottery works.

In 1901 London County Council purchased 200 acres of farmland to the east of White Hart Lane, but council house building did not start until 1920 with the building of the LCC 'cottage' estate. Other housing estates were built by Wood Green and Tottenham Councils south and east of the LCC estate, and have now extended to take over some of the older houses, such as Bradley Terrace.

Houses on the north side of White Hart Lane by Queen Street, Tottenham, in 1893, photographed looking westwards, by A. Little. The sign of the Three Compasses points the way to this public house in the narrow lane off Queen Street. The houses adjoined the grounds of St Katharine's College, a training institute for schoolmistresses, established by the Society for Promoting Christian Knowledge in 1878.

Modern-day Queen Street and White Hart Lane, with new housing. St Katharine's College later housed a Church of England school for girls, which moved to new buildings in Pretoria Road. The former training college's buildings are now part of the All Saints' campus of Middlesex University.

High Cross Road, Tottenham, 1893. Some of these weatherboarded cottages were rapidly becoming occupied by Eastern European immigrants, many of whom were Jewish. Positioned by the Hale, these houses offered cheap lodgings near the large manufacturing firms of Lebus, Gestetner and Flatau. More than one family often occupied the same small house and overcrowding was a problem. This led to the prosecution of some lodging-house keepers.

The dilapidated cottages were pulled down in about 1935 as part of the slum clearance objectives and other houses replaced them. Now a new arterial road – Monument Way – carves its way to the Hale through this once densely populated area. None the less, there remains a community spirit at High Cross in 2002.

The building of council houses, which covered much of the farmland in White Hart Lane in the 1930s, provided working-class families from London with good quality modern housing in spacious streets. This 1930s kitchen shows the deep butler sink, a wash boiler, gas cooker and water heater. This was exceptional luxury, as most of the residents of private rented housing would have had to make do with a coal-fired range for all their cooking and water heating.

At the turn of the twenty-first century Nicola Hunte washes up in her stainless steel sink with her daughter Pasha looking on. Nicola's house is part of a Housing Trust stock off White Hart Lane. Housing Trusts are taking over from local councils as providers of new social housing, although their housing schemes are usually smaller in size and do not create the big estates of the postwar council house-building.

5

Work & Commerce

The shops, workshops and industries in Tottenham and Wood Green in the nineteenth and twentieth centuries developed to supply the growing local population, as well as those of London and the South-East. This picture shows the workers of Samuel South and Sons Pottery, White Hart Lane, *c.* 1895. Samuel South, one of the sons, is standing to the right, wearing a bowler hat. These potteries were established in the mid-nineteenth century on local clayfields, and in 1896 were taken over by Samuel South. The business produced horticultural pots for nurseries using traditional hand-forming techniques. Alongside South's there were the Tottenham Potteries, owned by the Cole family and established in 1856. By the late 1950s changing production methods by competitors led to the closure of both potteries. The site of the two potteries is now St George's industrial estate.

Pearks corner shop on Philip Lane, shown here in about 1930 with a pile of newly laid eggs displayed in the window. Pearks was part of a chain, but most corner shops were family owned, offering an independent living in meeting the shopping needs of the local community. Pearks served the growing local community around Philip Lane. Its south side was bound by the densely packed nineteenth-century Victorian housing estates of South Tottenham, and to the north were the larger houses of the Edwardian Mount Pleasant estate.

Many corner shops have now disappeared, although some small shops continue, as we can see with the Aksu Supermarket on Philip Lane and its magnificent display of fruit and vegetables. The shops always demanded long hours of work from their owners, but not necessarily a reliable return from the poorer neighbourhoods. However, some continue to thrive, usually managed by hard-working and ambitious immigrants from Asia, Eastern Europe and the Middle East.

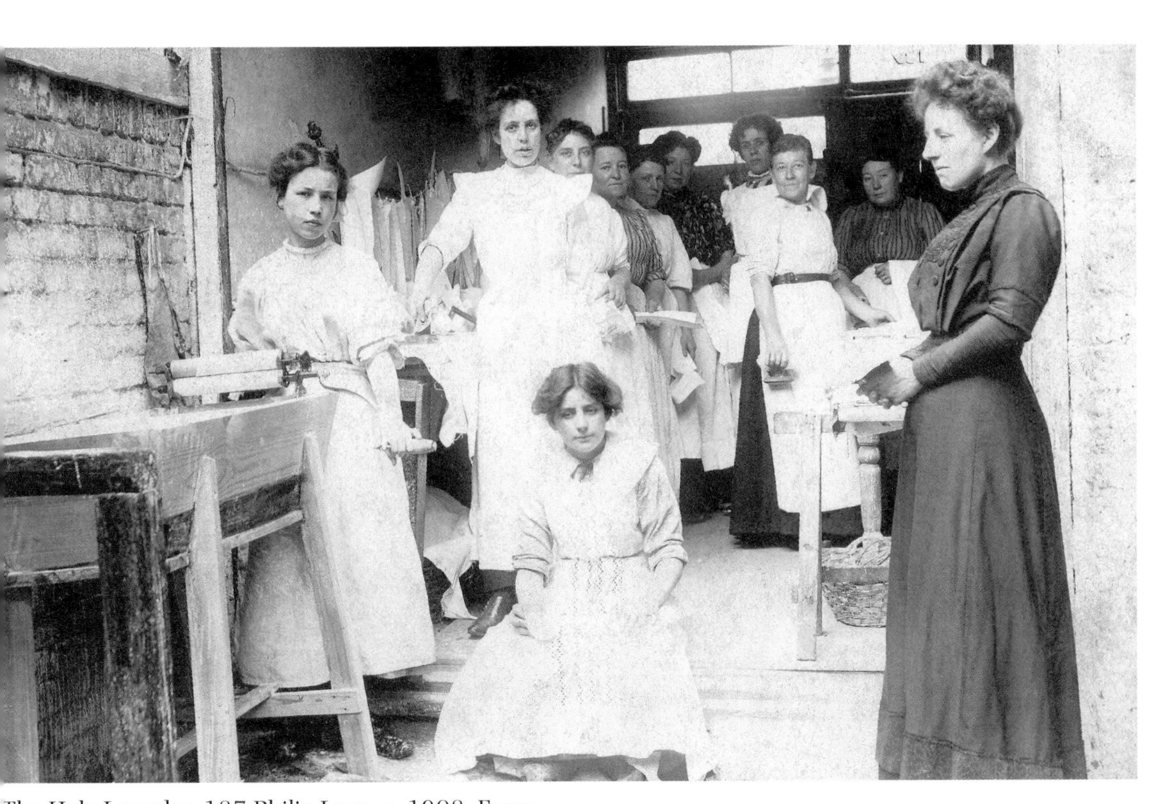

The Hale Laundry, 187 Philip Lane, *c.* 1908. From about 1903 Miss Lottie Hale ran her laundry business. She was a relative of local hero Sergeant Hale (see p. 29). Lottie is seen here dressed in black, posing with her employees. Apart from domestic service, laundry work was often the only opportunity available for young girls and women to contribute to their family's income. These premises were bare but functional with a wooden extension at the rear full of large scrubbing tubs, mangles and laundry baskets. In the scrubbing, mangling and ironing of laundry, these women endured work that was physically very demanding.

For about ten years the Hale laundry continued with Lottie in charge. The building remained a working laundry for the best part of the twentieth century. Nowadays Barnes and Partners, a firm of solicitors, occupies no. 187.

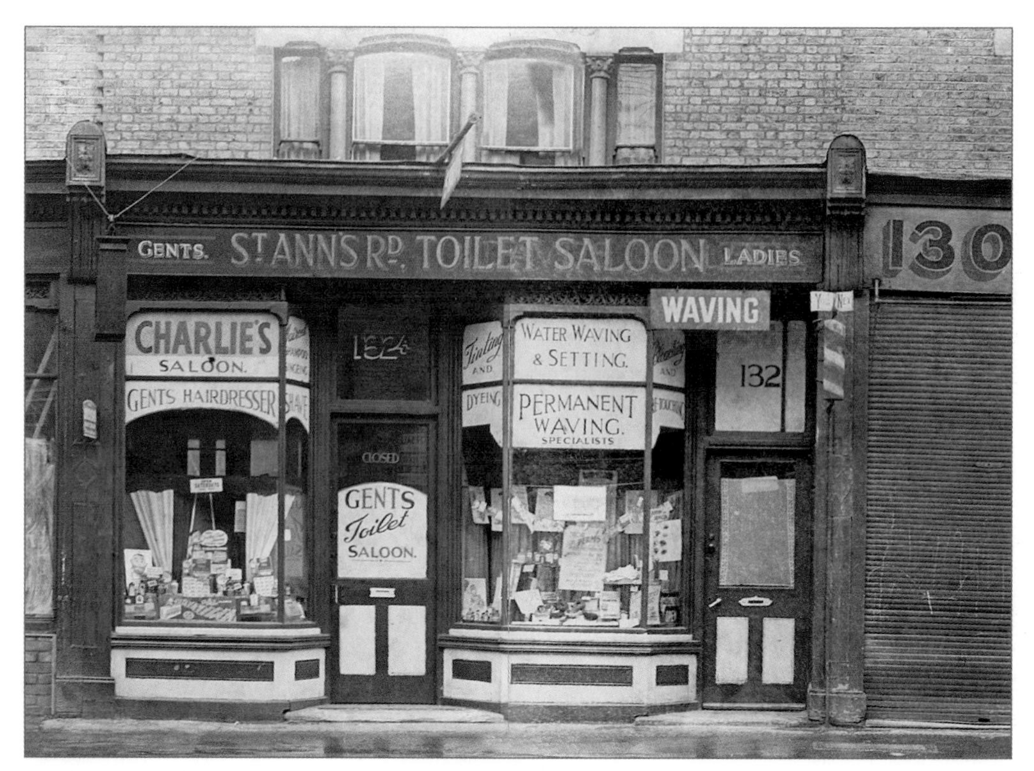

Hairdressing salon, 132 St Ann's Road, Tottenham, 23 August 1948. The first hairdresser to occupy this shop was Domenico Pasquale in 1910. By 1948 the salon was divided, with no. 132a operated by Simone, a ladies' hairdresser, and no. 132 by David Strauss, for gentlemen.

A hairdressing salon continued to operate from this site for the next twenty-five years until the terrace was pulled down to make way for new housing estates in St Ann's Road, during the 1970s and 1980s.

Daniel's Drug Stores on the corner of Canning Crescent and Wood Green High Road, *c.* 1900. Chemist shops dispensed many remedies and treatments for sickness and injuries, including ingredients for home-made medicine or the chemist's own formula. 'A patient would come in, ask to see the boss, describe his symptoms, and the boss would make up some medicine,' recalls David King, a chemist's assistant in the 1920s. Chemists also sold household products, including some very powerful ones for clearing drains or cleaning stains.

The modern health centre has replaced the chemist shop, but retained the health link. Opened in 1994, Canning Crescent Centre provides community mental health services, including offices, treatment and therapy, relocated following the closure of Friern Hospital in Barnet.

Scotland Green in February 1906, photographed by Fred Fisk. The buildings of Tottenham High Road can be seen in the distance. Local unemployed men have been put to work on the culverting of the Moselle brook. As Fisk writes: 'The Moselle . . . had been a great source of trouble and annoyance from time immemorial', with Tottenham often experiencing severe flooding. From 1836 onwards sections of the brook were covered to help avert further problems.

Originating in Muswell Hill, the Moselle now runs underground through Haringey and only surfaces at Tottenham Cemetery and Lordship Recreation Ground. At Scotland Green the brook once flowed through on the north side, via Carbuncle or Garbell Ditch, through to the Marshes and the River Lea. This is now Carbuncle Alley. Today the job centre marks the entrance to Scotland Green.

Barratt's Sweet Factory in Mayes Road, shown here in 1902, was one of the most important factories in Wood Green. Established in 1848 in Islington by George Barratt, the firm moved to Wood Green in 1880 and these offices were opened in 1897. Starting as a family business, it eventually became a large public company and at its peak it provided nearly 1,000 jobs. It also offered housing for some of its workers; one road nearby is called Barratt Avenue.

Barratt's closed in 1980, after having been taken over by the Bassett Group in 1966, but some of its buildings remain in use. The office block is now Cambridge House, occupied by the Metropolitan Housing Trust. The factory has become part of Wood Green industrial area, with light industries and small businesses, as well as the chocolate factory which accommodates workshops for local artists and artisans.

W.T. Williamson and Sons' pottery works on Green Lanes, alongside Harringay Park station, was a run-down and unsanitary place at the time these photographs were taken in 1905, with stagnant ponds and muddy fields. The clay workings had been established on this site of Bean's Green from 1798 and the cottages were built in 1843. This house and the premises were condemned by the Medical Officer of Health as unfit for habitation in 1905, and so were closed.

Harringay Dog Stadium, one of the first in London, was opened on the Williamson's Potteries site in 1927. It was able to accommodate 50,000 spectators, and in 1921 speedway racing was introduced, followed by stock-car racing in the 1960s. It eventually closed in 1987. Next to the site was Harringay Arena, opened in 1936, holding major boxing fixtures and shows until it closed in 1958. The stadium and arena sites have now been redeveloped for large stores, including the Sainsbury's superstore shown here.

In 1908 the Wood Green Dust Destructor was opened in Western Road on the site of the Old Moat House on Wood Green Common, behind the swimming baths. It was then a state-of-the-art processor for the urban waste being produced by a growing community. Most of this waste was usually reduced to ashes (the 'dust'), as residents used to burn their rubbish in their own fireplaces. There was also substantially less food waste then because people shopped daily for food as they needed it.

After becoming a refuse incinerator in the 1960s, the Wood Green depot eventually closed, and the huge quantities of local rubbish are now directed towards the vast Edmonton incinerator on the North Circular. Burning rubbish in an incinerator or disposing of it in landfill sites have serious implications for the environment, but this recycling unit on the same Western Road is somewhat more environment friendly.

Palace Gates Road in 1906 shows a variety of businesses, including an oilman's and ironmonger's, chemist's and drapery shop, catering for a growing local community. The road, at the bottom of Alexandra Palace Hill, was built between 1894 and 1912 at the same time as the houses along Crescent, Dagmar and Victoria Roads, on land that was formerly part of Nightingale Hall Farm. Nearby Wood Green and Palace Gates stations provided easy access to central London and the City.

The ironmonger's shop no longer spills out on to the pavement, but there is still a thriving parade of shops and businesses, in particular cafés and restaurants as well as a post office and plant and flower shop. The frontage of the upper storeys also remains much the same.

Commerce Road, seen here in about 1906, was at the southern end of Wood Green's earliest building development from the 1850s, including Finsbury, Truro, Clarence and Nightingale Roads. Commerce Road, as its name indicated, provided the local community with many of its shops and amenities, including a Saturday open-air market. There was also a considerable amount of industry and small workshops here, such as a saddler's, coach-builder's, printer's, clock manufacturer's and a large garage. Syrees Garage accommodated seven independent bus operators between 1924 and 1931, and continued as a garage until the 1970s redevelopment.

By the late 1950s the streets around Commerce Road were regarded as undesirable for residential use and were part of a clearance programme by Wood Green UDC. The old houses, surrounded by shops and industries, were often overcrowded, and the council favoured a new development of more modern, cleaner and more spacious homes. Inevitably these were in blocks of flats, and they also displaced the shops and workshops that had provided both employment and amenities for the local residents.

Finsbury Road with Wood Green Baptist church tucked in behind the railings in the middle of the picture, 1905. Finsbury Road used to run from Trinity Road to Truro Road until the clearance programme. Finsbury Road is named after the Finsbury Freehold Land Society, which acquired the land of Wood Green Farm in 1853 to develop the Commerce Road Estate. Like Commerce Road, it also had its share of shops and workshops, and alongside the church we find a laundry, blind-makers, tailors, boot-maker and house-furnisher.

Finsbury Road was cut in two by the building of Nightingale Primary School during the 1970s redevelopment. The shops in the above picture have disappeared, and have been replaced by the trees around the school (now Haringey Pupil Support Centre), leaving these Victorian cottages. The taller houses at the end have been converted from the former shops.

Another commercial artery in north Wood Green is Myddleton Road, seen here in 1908. On the border of Palmers Green, it runs from the High Road to Bowes Park station and is on land that was once part of Bowes Farm Manor Estate. The Bowes Park Estate, partly in Wood Green and partly in Palmers Green, was developed in the 1870s, and given a further boost when Bowes Park station opened in 1880. The shops here include a tailor's, grocery, printer's and a photographer's.

Myddelton Road today still has a range of small shops and business, although some have reverted to housing stock in this mixed residential and business road. The name of the road derives from Sir Hugh Myddelton, the seventeenth-century engineer who brought fresh water to London through the construction of the New River. In the 1850s a tunnel was built between Myddelton Road and Station Road to take the river and shorten its length. The land above the tunnel has become the open spaces of Finsbury Gardens, Nightingale Gardens and part of Avenue Gardens.

Harry Carter stands next to his horse, Sampson, in Victoria Road, *c.* 1932. Harry, who made two deliveries a day – even on Christmas Day – one for fresh milk and the second for fruit and vegetables, came from Ireland, and worked for United Dairies from 1925 until 1962, receiving many medals for good service. He was the last milkman in Wood Green to continue to use a horse. His granddaughter recalls he was devastated when his last horse was taken away while he was on holiday. The United Dairies depot was then in Station Road, built on the premises that used to belong to Abbott Brothers dairy farmers.

A van rather than a milk float is used to deliver milk today, usually to local shops, as we can see from this delivery outside Best Wines store along Church Hill in Wood Green High Road.

Jnredeemed goods in Russell's, pawnbroker's,
488 Tottenham High Road, *c.* 1865.
Neighbouring the George & Vulture pub, the
ign of the three gold balls was a common sight.
Along with the 'Tally shop' (selling goods on
credit), this was part of everyday life. As one
ocal recalls: 'It was tough for everybody. I'll be
ruthful. My mother used to have to go to the
pawnshop. My dad had a "Tally-man". He paid
nim so much a week. If we missed one week he
ised to come round. People would dodge him
and hide behind the curtains.'

Paradise Gems, jeweller and pawnbroker,
536 Tottenham High Road, 2002.

J. Drobchinsky, hair frame manufacturer, 679 Seven Sisters Road, Tottenham, *c.* 1920. Like other Jewish immigrants moving to Tottenham at the turn of the twentieth century, Mr Drobchinsky started work in the area around the High Cross, at 17 Colsterworth Road. His business responded to the requirements of the Orthodox Jewish community, in particular providing wigs for married women.

Beauty Queen's Cosmetics, Afro and European hair and beauty store, 487 Tottenham High Road, 2002. The presence of such specialist shops today owes much to the determination and success of local firm Dyke & Dryden Ltd. Building a business to satisfy the growing demand for suitable grooming products, Dyke & Dryden became Europe's largest Black haircare and cosmetics company, which was established in Tottenham in 1965. Directors Tony Wade, Len Dyke and Dudley Dryden were a respected pioneering partnership for the Black business community in the UK.

6

The Community

William 'Billy' Mudge, seen here in about 1950, was a well-known Tottenham character and a lifelong supporter of Tottenham Hotspur Football Club. One of Tottenham's first motorists, at the end of the nineteenth century he established a car-hire firm for weddings, funerals and other events at premises in Tottenham High Road near the football ground. It is unlikely he hired out his antique bike, although it is recorded that he allowed Spurs fans to leave their bicycles in his yard for a small fee. Many local residents recall the notice outside the narrow entrance to his garage: 'Slow down to 60 mph up this gateway'. Mudge was one of many in Tottenham who opened up successful new businesses in the area, some of them staying as family firms and others expanding into public companies.

Preparing to 'beat the bounds' at the site of the former Old Blue Lion Tavern on the Tottenham/Edmonton parish boundary, *c.* 1890. This ancient custom was performed to check boundary markers and traditionally to beat out evil spirits with the 'sacred' willow rods. Gathering at the Blue Lion was near the point where many past perambulations of the parish of Tottenham began. Processions were always celebrated with a drink!

Increasing urbanisation and the presence of permanent boundary markers saw the practice of beating the bounds come to an end in 1893. Since the reorganisation of local government in 1965, a Haringey Council sign has marked the modern-day boundary between the two London boroughs of Haringey and Enfield where the Tottenham High Road meets Upper Fore Street, Edmonton.

Tottenham Carnival passing by Scotland Green in 1902. In 1899 cycling clubs in Tottenham (followed by Ward Committees) organised the first carnival parades, raising money for the Tottenham Hospital (later the Prince of Wales Hospital) and other local causes. In 1902 the procession left Tottenham Hale at 4 p.m. and proceeded around each Ward up the High Road to Edmonton. The torchlit procession returned to Tottenham Green by 8.15 p.m.

Tottenham Carnival Parade in June 2002. The carnival parade was revived in 1998 by Haringey Arts Council with Councillors Sheila Peacock and Kyriakos Fiakkas and local Tottenham traders. Since then each summer has seen thousands flock to enjoy the music, dance and delicious food representative of many countries at the Community Festival in Bruce Castle Park and Museum. (*Picture courtesy of Tony Gay*)

A modern-day school outing by coach.

Pub outing by brake from the Green Gate public house, by Willow Walk and West Green Road, *c.* 1905. Among this men-only group is Mr Fuller (whose family owned the photograph), standing next to the young girl. Great pleasure could be had on day trips and outings. Often these were the only 'holidays' that many families could afford. The Green Gate has been a pub since 1862 and, after a 1931 rebuild by the Stag Brewery, is still in business under the same name today.

REID
SMOKE

The children of Lancasterian Infant School pose for this formal portrait in their hall in 1908. They are seated behind their classroom desks, which have been moved into the hall for the picture. These are the same desks they would have sat at throughout the school day. Some of the children are showing their work on slates. The school was built by Tottenham School Board in 1887, absorbing the old Lancasterian Boys' School (established 1812) and Lancasterian Girls' School (established 1815).

A modern assembly in the same hall is considerably more informal, although the hall itself has changed little. Mrs Alison Maynard (centre) is showing the work from one of the classes to the school, with the children alongside her. The school now has a resource base located on the site, which caters for physical disability and includes a hydrotherapy pool and rooms for physiotherapy.

Wood Green Higher Grade Board School for Boys and Girls, shown here in 1903, was opened in 1899. Before the 1944 Act introduced secondary education for all, the higher grade schools offered secondary education for pupils who were not selected for a grammar school place. In 1921, it became Trinity County Mixed Grammar School, and then in 1968 the upper school for St Thomas More Catholic School, following comprehensive reorganisation in Haringey.

In the 1990s the upper and lower schools of St Thomas More were rehoused in the former Wood Green County School in Glendale Avenue and the Trinity Road building transferred to Nightingale Primary School. Nightingale was formerly in modern premises built following the Commerce Road development, but the building eventually became too small for the increasing numbers of pupils.

Fire patrol from Dongola Road, Tottenham, in 1941. During the Second World War these volunteers were the core fighters in the event of a fire, with the subsidiary support from firewatchers. They pose with hand-held stirrup pumps needed for putting out small fires caused by incendiary bombs.

Present-day firemen from White Watch at Tottenham Fire Station in St Loy's Road. Pictured from left to right are fire-fighters Simon Kleman, Stuart Haigh, Alan Harris, Jon Thornton (Station Officer), Tim Kingsven, Stanford Clarke and kneeling, Joe Horner and Geoff Meager. In 2002 the fire service entered into a dispute with the government over pay deals for firefighters.

The Public Baths at High Cross Parade, west side of Tottenham High Road, 1890. This was a commercial enterprise operated by the Colman family.

Following the Baths and Washhouses Act of 1893, the local authority began building Tottenham's central baths in 1904, next to the newly built fire station in Town Hall Approach. This included slipper baths and two swimming baths. Although Colman's bath house has long gone, some original buildings from the parade can still be seen.

Friends' Meeting House, 594 Tottenham High Road, with a hoarding advertising Burgess's Stores next door, 1949. In 1715 Tottenham's significant Quaker community built their first meeting house here, alongside the old Sanchez Almshouses (see p. 21). Members included the American William Dillwyn, Josiah Forster and Priscilla Wakefield, the earliest supporters of the Anti-Slavery Movement in this country.

The meeting house was rebuilt in 1809 to accommodate the increasing numbers of Quakers settling in Tottenham. By 1956 their population was dwindling, and by 1962 shops and offices were built on the site. A smaller meeting house was constructed above the shops; it still serves its community today. The former burial ground of the Friends can be found on land to the rear of the building.

Wesleyan chapel, Tottenham High Road, by the photographer Hunnings, *c*. 1870. Originally holding meetings in a barn, in 1817 local Methodists in Tottenham built their first Wesleyan chapel opposite Bruce Grove. It could seat up to 400 people. By the 1860s the chapel was becoming inadequate and a new church accommodating 1,000 people was planned further along the road. The old chapel was almost destroyed by fire in 1882. The site was then occupied by the offices of the builders' merchants G.L. Wilson & Co. Ltd.

The second Wesleyan chapel was erected in 1867 on land acquired from the Forster family (Forster Road now runs alongside the church). By 1937 the chapel's spire was becoming unstable. During the Second World War two land mines exploded nearby, causing additional structural damage. Because of financial constraints, the rebuilding of a new Methodist church was incorporated into a shopping parade along the High Road. It was opened in 1963 and dedicated to St Mark. Today neighbouring shops include Crazy Cuts the hairdressers and the old firm of A. Seaward, the undertakers.

The Salvation Army opened its Citadel on the corner of Mayes Road and Alexandra Road in 1890, having had a barracks in Finsbury Road from 1886. This picture, taken in 1910, shows the busy street market that was part of the shops and stalls of these two roads (see p. 47). Inside the Citadel there was a hall able to seat 700 people, with a gallery on three sides and a stage on the fourth side.

The old Citadel, along with the open-fronted shops and stalls, was demolished in the mid-1970s to make way for the new shopping centre. This new meeting place has moved away from the nineteenth-century barracks and Citadel to become the Salvation Army Wood Green Christian Centre. It opened in 1976 in Lymington Avenue, across the road from Mayes Road.

Holy Trinity Church and Green School, Tottenham Green, 26 October 1894. The new extension of the school had just been completed when A. Little took this photograph. The school, which takes its name from the children's green uniforms, opened in 1847. Outside the walls stands the old parish pump, which once supplied most inhabitants of Tottenham with water. In 1883 the water was considered unfit to drink, so the pump was chained up.

The church was consecrated in 1830. At the time of construction its design by James Savage received high praise, and today this is recognised in its listed status. The original pinnacles have been lost, but these could be reinstated under a future restoration programme. In 2003 the old pump is about to undergo repair to its fabric.

Trinity chapel, Trinity Road, in 1903, which had opened as a Wesleyan Methodist chapel in 1871. Before the chapel was built the Methodists held open-air meetings on the green between Trinity Road and Bounds Green Road. The building of the chapel was aided by a fund established to promote the erection of fifty Wesleyan chapels in London.

The church in Trinity Road looks much the same here, its outline still softened by trees. Since 1970 it has been the Greek Orthodox Cathedral of St Mary's. In 1980 there was a serious fire, but the cathedral was rebuilt on the same lines as its predecessor. The change of use reflects the numbers of Greek families who moved into Wood Green and Palmers Green.

The Baptist church in Finsbury Road, round the corner from the Wesleyan chapel, was opened in 1875. In 1907 it moved to larger premises in Braemar Avenue and the building was converted to the Catholic Apostolic Church. In 1965 it again changed to become the Greek Orthodox Church of St Barnabas.

The old church has been dramatically changed from a sombre, ivy-clad Baptist building in the nineteenth century to the Mediterranean white of the twenty-first-century Greek Orthodox church. The surroundings have also changed substantially. Whereas it used to be tucked between a row of shops in the main thoroughfare of Finsbury Road, leading from Bounds Green to Nightingale Road, it now ends in a pleasant cul-de-sac.

Tottenham Hebrew Congregation religion class, *c.* 1912. In 1904 less than twenty Jewish families lived in Tottenham, mainly near Colsterworth Road. Observing the Jewish faith, they initially met in each other's homes for prayers. They later rented a room for religious education classes at the Home and Hospital for 'Jewish Incurables' on the High Road. As the Jewish community grew, by 1911 they established a synagogue for the Tottenham Hebrew Congregation, renting the building of the former Clarion Workingmen's Club at 366 Tottenham High Road. In 1912 over seventy local Jewish families were members.

After the Second World War membership dramatically increased, peaking in 1954 with 435 families. Since then Jewish families have gradually moved away from the area. In recent years use of the synagogue has declined, and in 2002 the building was sold for redevelopment. In February 2003 a full membership attended a valedictory service at the synagogue.

The Bull Inn public house, 278 Tottenham High Road, on 23 October 1892. Photographer A. Little has snapped the brewer's dray and horse standing on the road with its delivery. This old inn could boast fleeting associations with royalty; its name was first recorded by Henry VIII in 1537. Over 300 years later a sign would hang over the door at the Bull to indicate that Queen Victoria had stopped there in 1856 on her way to Epping Forest.

In the twentieth century the Bull was one of the oldest inns left standing in its original state. Although it has been mainly rebuilt, it is one of the few pubs on the High Road still to be set back from the road. It is now known as the Connaught Tavern and may be described as an Irish-style bar.

The Red Lion public house, 634 Tottenham High Road, *c.* 1867. During the seventeenth century this was one of the noted inns of Tottenham. This view shows the proprietor's name as W. Mattocks. The bystanders include two policemen and a member of the local militia from the 33rd Middlesex (Tottenham) Volunteer Rifle Corps. In 1869, to make way for the building of Lansdowne Road, the pub was removed and rebuilt slightly to the south by builder James Linzell, who lived in one of the houses next door.

With a billiard's room and a furnished club room, from the early twentieth century the new Red Lion pub was the meeting headquarters for several groups including the Tottenham Wheelers and the Eagle Angling Society. A popular High Road pub today, the Red Lion occupies the same building and was refurbished in 2002.

The George & Vulture public house, 490 Tottenham High Road, 1910. During the late sixteenth century the ancient gabled house was home to Balthazar Sanchez, wealthy Spanish confectioner and local benefactor. On becoming a hostelry and inn, its rural setting, gardens, bowling green, fishpond and stables were a favourite haunt for visitors. In 1797 the Marquis de Longchamps and his wife lived here in poverty as refugees from the French Revolution. By 1807 the house was a boarding school, but by 1829 it had fallen into such disrepair it was demolished.

From the 1860s the new George & Vulture public house would stand for another century. Replacement buildings on this ancient drinking spot have included both Fine Fare and the Kwik Save supermarket chains.

A reception following the opening ceremony of Bounds Green fire station in 1914, including many of the local dignitaries of Wood Green Urban District Council who initiated its building. The station had an engine house and training tower, and also operated a motor ambulance. Six firemen's flats were included with the station, with a further six built in 1924.

In 1963, now part of the London Fire Brigade, the fire station was closed with the building of new fire stations at Tottenham, Hornsey and Southgate. The building is now an ambulance station, with the firemen's houses no longer occupied by the firemen and their families.

INDEX